UNDERSTANDING WATER BAPTISM

Understanding Water Baptism

David Pawson

Anchor Recordings

Copyright © 1992, 2015, 2017 David Pawson

The right of David Pawson to be identified as author of this Work has been asserted by him in accordance with the Copyright, Designs and Patents Act 1988.

First published in Great Britain in 1992.
Revised and published in 2015 under the title Explaining Water Baptism.
This edition published in 2017 by Anchor Recordings Ltd
DPTT, Synegis House, 21 Crockhamwell Road, Woodley, Reading RG5 3LE

No part of this publication may be reproduced or transmitted in any form or by any means, electronic or mechanical, including photocopy, recording or any information storage and retrieval system, without prior permission in writing from the publisher.

**For more of David Pawson's teaching,
including DVDs and CDs, go to
www.davidpawson.com**

**FOR FREE DOWNLOADS
www.davidpawson.org**

**For further information, email
info@davidpawsonministry.com**

Unless otherwise indicated,
Scripture quotations taken from the
HOLY BIBLE, NEW INTERNATIONAL VERSION.
Copyright © 1973, 1978, 1984 by International Bible Society.
Used by permission of Hodder & Stoughton Publishers,
a member of the Hachette Livre UK Group. All rights reserved.
"NIV" is a registered trademark of International Bible Society.
UK trademark number 1448790.

USA acknowledgement:
Scriptures taken from the
Holy Bible, New International Version®, NIV®.
Copyright © 1973, 1978, 1984, 2011 by Biblica, Inc.™
Used by permission of Zondervan. All rights reserved worldwide.
www.zondervan.com
The "NIV" and "New International Version" are trademarks registered
in the United States Patent and Trademark Office by Biblica, Inc.™

ISBN 978-1-911173-24-3

Printed by Lightning Source

Contents

	Introduction	7
1.	A matter of life and death	9
2.	A very peculiar practice	13
3.	Dirty people need a bath	19
4.	Dead people need a burial	25
5.	A case of identification	29
6.	What's in a name?	35
7.	Penitent believers only	39
8.	Water and Spirit	45
9.	The church door	51
10.	Symbol or sacrament?	59
11.	Baptism saves you now	65
12.	Baby or believer?	71

INTRODUCTION

A hole is cut in the ice on a frozen lake in Siberia. A woman is gently lowered into it until the chilling water closes over her head. Quickly pulled out again, she walks some distance to a nearby cottage, her clothes freezing solid on the way. Thawed out in front of a log fire, she joins her companions in a celebration.

In drought-stricken India a grave is dug. It is lined with a white cotton sheet, on which a living man is laid. The cloth is drawn over him and sprinkled with precious drops of water until it is soaked. Then it is flung aside and the man is lifted out to share in a festivity with his friends.

In different countries and climates, the same thing is happening all over the world – at a rate of over fifty a minute, three thousand an hour, about seventy thousand a day. In streams, rivers, the sea and artificial pools, large or small, people are being immersed in water, apparently bringing great happiness to both the participants and the spectators.

What is going on? If you asked them, they would tell you that this is what is called "baptism". Why do they do it? They would tell you they are obeying Jesus Christ, the Son of God. How do they know he wants them to do this? They will point you to their scriptures, the Bible – and especially the second section of it, the New Testament.

That is what we are going to look at in this book. I will try to explain what "water-baptism" is all about by examining what Jesus and his apostles both said and did about it. While this will be the primary focus of our study, we shall have to take notice of how the Christian church has applied (and misapplied!) their teaching and practice over the last two thousand years.

UNDERSTANDING WATER BAPTISM

You will find many Bible references (with the book, chapter, and verse numbers in brackets). It would be a mistake to look all these up during your first reading of the book; that would interrupt the flow of thought in your mind. But you will probably want to check up on some of the more surprising statements.

Sometimes, alas, the Bible and the church say different things. We have to choose between them, which can be painful and disturbing. This is particularly true for the subject of baptism, as we shall see. But for followers of Jesus, the issue is clear – we are not to nullify the word of God by our traditions (Mark 7:13).

Baptism can be costly. I lost my job, my house and my pension over it. Some have even lost their lives, in countries dominated by a religion which regards conversion to Christianity as treason.

Perhaps I'd better warn you before you read any further! You cannot just go through a book like this out of mere curiosity or academic interest. You will have to search your own heart as well as the scriptures to know where you stand on the matter. It is difficult, perhaps impossible, to remain neutral.

For baptism is neither optional nor peripheral to the Christian life. It is fundamental to our personal relationship with the Lord Jesus and, therefore, to our eternal salvation.

Note: Some of the content of this book, though no actual material, comes from my much fuller study of Christian initiation, entitled *The Normal Christian Birth*, by kind permission of the publishers (Hodder and Stoughton). Pastors, evangelists and church workers are urged to obtain a copy, which looks at the subject in much greater depth. A video version is available from Anchor Recordings, 72 The Street, Kennington, Ashford, Kent TN24 9HS, UK.

1

A MATTER OF LIFE AND DEATH

Without water, life on earth would be impossible. The amount of water on our planet makes it unique among the countless bodies hurtling around the universe. From one point in space, above the Pacific Ocean, it looks as if it is all water. The Bible says it once was. Seashells at the top of our highest mountains confirm this.

The main component of our bodies is also water. We can survive without food longer than without drink. Without water we would have no food: light and moisture are essential to its production. When sun and rain come together, the resulting rainbow is God's reminder that he has promised to maintain the supply of both as long as the earth is still here.

Drinking and cooking are not the biggest demand on our water supply. Keeping clean is the major usage. We wash our bodies, our clothes, our dishes, our windows, our cars and a host of things. Inventing washing machines for many of these functions has greatly increased our need for water as has the explosion in world population. The shortage of clean, fresh water is becoming a serious threat to the survival of the human race.

Washing dirt away is a pleasure as well as a necessity. It feels good to be clean. A bath or shower can lift our spirits. The opposite is also true: it feels bad to be dirty. That is why some people develop an obsession for washing hands frequently and others a phobia about contamination. Sometimes washing the body is thought to be a cure for moral guilt. (One thinks of Pontius Pilate and his futile attempt to "wash his hands" of Jesus, after condemning him to be crucified in spite of finding him innocent – little did he dream that his name would be included in Christian creeds down the ages – Matthew 27:24.)

Not surprisingly, ceremonial washing or ritual baths have figured in human history. A bridegroom may thus be cleansed before his wedding, a worshipper before he says his prayers or a priest before he offers a sacrifice. It is a recognition that something pure must not be polluted. The act of ablution is believed to deal with more than physical dirt; it is intended to remove all possible sources of defilement.

We have almost reached the point of beginning to understand Christian baptism, but first we must consider another side to the character of water. We have looked at the way it supports life, but it can also destroy life!

Sometimes this is due to its *quality*, or lack of it. Polluted water is a notorious carrier of disease. Untreated sewage and chemical waste can cause havoc. Plagues and epidemics spread rapidly when the water supply is disrupted and contaminated.

Often, it is due to the *quantity*. Hurricanes and earthquakes can produce tidal waves which cause loss of life, as well as damage to property. The narrowing rain-belts around our globe increase the threat of floods, as well as drought.

Yet even when the oceans stay within their bounds, they represent a serious danger to human life. Though human beings have conquered the sea by sailing over it in ships and under it in submarines, the sea has often conquered them. The seabed is littered with wrecked vessels and the remains of drowned sailors (even the Titanic, of which it was arrogantly claimed that "God himself could not sink her"). On the day of resurrection, the sea will give up its myriad dead (Revelation 20:13).

Many people, therefore, fear the water, even to the

degree of a paralysing terror, called hydrophobia. This is not inherited but comes from some unfortunate experience or association. It can cause panic at the prospect of baptism, though many have found in the event that they were cured of it!

The Jewish people were not historically fond of the water. Unlike the neighbouring Phoenicians, who pioneered navigation by the stars and regularly sailed as far as England for tin, Israel did not even have any ships until King Solomon started a navy. They would probably be pleased to learn that in the new earth God is going to create, there will be *"no more sea"* (Revelation 21:1).

Water played a vital role in Israel's history. Two quite spectacular events were engraved in their national memory, one of which is re-enacted in an annual festival to this very day. Both are directly related to baptism in the New Testament. Significantly, they were quite literally matters of life and death. Or rather, death and life – for that is the order in the Bible, particularly in relation to Jesus (Revelation 1:18).

The first was the widespread flood in the days of Noah. A world polluted by perverted sex and unrestrained violence so offended God that he regretted having created independent human beings (Genesis 6:6 is probably the saddest verse in the Bible). He resolved to wash the filth away by releasing torrential rain and tidal waves (Genesis 7:11). Yet one family of eight, led by a good father, was saved from the deluge by building a covered raft exactly according to God's instructions. The waters which drowned everybody else actually carried them through the disaster to a clean world in which human history could have a new beginning. Little wonder that Peter saw in this saga a clear analogy for Christian baptism (1 Peter 3:20–21).

The second was the miraculous escape from Egypt in the

days of Moses. Trapped between Pharaoh's army and the Red (or Reed) Sea, the two and a half million Hebrew refugees faced possible slaughter or certain slavery. Providentially (the word means "God provided"), a strong wind parted the shallow channel and a cloud hid their flight across its bed. The same waters protecting their flanks closed on their pursuers, drowning the entire force. This amazing deliverance sealed both their liberty from Pharaoh and their loyalty to Moses. Paul says they were *"baptized into Moses"* (1 Corinthians 10:2), using them as an example for those who are delivered from Satan and *"baptized into Christ"* (Galatians 3:27; more of this in Chapter 5).

Apart from these noteworthy deliverances, which prefigure baptism, baptism is never directly mentioned in the Old Testament. The nearest thing to it would be the practice of bathing the priests before they undertook their holy duties in the tabernacle and later the temple (Leviticus 8:6). Some claim a parallel in the circumcision of male babies on the eighth day (and thereby justify infant baptism); but this was not for the purpose of cleansing. It is never linked with baptism in the New Testament, even though circumcision was the subject of the biggest debate in the early church. It belongs to Jewish flesh, not Christian faith.

We have exhausted all that the Old Testament can tell us about this "very peculiar practice" of baptism. If there is little about it in the Old, however, there is much in the New.

2

A VERY PECULIAR PRACTICE

In most parts of the world, the word "baptize" is almost exclusively used as a religious term to describe a church ceremony. Water always plays a part, but the amount of it varies enormously – from a little put on the head to the whole body put in a lot!

Those without any knowledge of the Greek language may be forgiven for not knowing that it was, and still is, a quite ordinary word used in everyday life. It is used whenever a solid is submerged in a liquid. A cup is "baptized" in a bowl of wine to fill it; a piece of cloth is "baptized" in a vat of dye. A ship is "baptized", not when it is launched for its first voyage, but when it is sunk on its last!

There are many equivalent words in the English language: to dip, to plunge, to duck, to douse. "Immerse" comes as near as any. The essential element is the total contact between the solid and the liquid. If the solid is absorbent, then "soak" or "saturate" would be appropriate (though this is clearly not the case with the human body).

Most English versions of the Bible fail to translate the Greek verb into any of these easily understood equivalent terms. Instead, it is usually transliterated – spelled out in English letters, but unchanged in form. This has effectively concealed its natural meaning of "immerse" and allowed the word to be applied to pouring (called "affusion") or even a little sprinkling.

Apart from contradicting the meaning of the word, these

latter modes are neither in line with the New Testament practice (which we shall look at now) nor in tune with New Testament significance (as we shall see in the next two chapters). In the apostolic writings, baptism is the momentary submerging of the whole body in water (Matthew 3:16; John 3:23; Acts 8:38).

When did this act of cleansing acquire a spiritual purpose? A man called John was the first to be called "the baptizer" (or, as we would say, "the plunger" or "the dipper"), which seems to suggest that he was the first to do such an extraordinary thing.

Some would argue that he only took over an existing Jewish practice called proselyte baptism, used when a Gentile wanted to become a naturalised Jewish citizen. A father and his sons would be circumcised, then he and his whole family would be immersed as well, to symbolically wash away all taint of their pagan past. Subsequent babies were not bathed, for they were considered born as Jews, though males would still be circumcised.

The problem is that the earliest evidence for this is found long after John. Jesus, the apostles and the early church were already doing it – so we don't know for sure who got it from whom. If John's candidates were already familiar with proselyte baptism, then they were being told they were no better than pagan Gentiles in God's sight and needed to have their lives cleaned up just as much!

Turning from speculation to certainties, we know that John immersed thousands in the river Jordan as the central feature of his mission to prepare the people of Israel for their coming King (in Hebrew – Messiah; in Greek – Christ). It is also clear that he saw it in moral terms, insisting on confession of sins and proof of reformation before he immersed them. We may deduce from this that he only accepted those who had committed sins and knew that they were to blame for them. Children under twelve would not be included, since their parents were considered morally responsible for their behaviour. A further point to note is that it was an individual responsibility – no one could confess or be baptized vicariously for another.

In plunging Jews into these muddy waters at the lowest point of the earth's surface, John had chosen a very meaningful location. This was the very place where their forefathers, after escaping from Egypt and wandering forty years in the desert, had crossed into the Promised Land. It was as if he was telling them they had to begin all over again – but this time starting clean.

It is also a fact of history that Jesus himself was baptized. John, who was actually his cousin, refused at first to immerse him. He had rejected others who refused to repent of their sins, but his reason in this case was the exact opposite – Jesus had no sins to confess! Already he was acknowledged to be unique. John wanted to be baptized by Jesus (revealing that the first baptizer was not baptized himself!). Jesus, however, insisted, thus robbing his followers of any excuse which regards baptism as unnecessary.

After he began his own ministry, Jesus continued the practice of immersion. Indeed, at one stage he and John were doing the same thing just a few miles apart on the same river. Some cynics tried to drive a wedge between them by pointing out that Jesus' baptisms were proving more popular than John's. The reply says much about John's character as well as his calling: "He's the bridegroom; I'm just the best man. He must get more attention while I must get less" (John 3:22–30; my paraphrase).

The record carefully points out that Jesus delegated the actual immersing to his disciples, probably to avoid odious comparisons based on who administered it. Note that Peter and Paul exercised the same discretion after they became famous (Acts 10:48; 1 Corinthians 1:14). The identity of the baptizer should not be the focus of attention, and the act of baptism forges no special tie with the one baptizing.

After the first few months, the practice seems to have faded into the background of Jesus' public ministry (or at least was not considered worthy of mention by the Gospel writers). After Jesus had died and risen again, however, he gave it even greater prominence. Before returning to heaven, he gave his followers their "marching orders" for a worldwide mission. They were to make disciples in every nation (ethnic group rather than political state) on earth. They were to do this in two steps – first, by immersing them; second, by teaching them to live in the way Jesus had instructed (Matthew 28:19–20).

It is no surprise, therefore, to find that on the day of Pentecost, when Peter's first-ever public preaching brought a huge response, the enquirers were told to *"repent and be baptized* [immersed]*"* (Acts 2:38). The pools of Bethesda and Siloam were within easy reach and someone interested in numbers counted three thousand baptisms on that first day of the church's mission. From then on, baptism has continued to be the universal practice of the Christian church – though in form, meaning and application it has often been changed beyond recognition.

In other words, there is scarcely any evidence of an unbaptized Christian in the New Testament. That would have seemed like a contradiction in terms. Baptism was an integral element in obeying the gospel (2 Thessalonians 1:8). It would have been inconceivable to claim to be a disciple of Jesus while not fulfilling his command or following his example in this way. The letters of Paul, Peter and others to early believers assume as a matter of course that all their readers have been baptized and can recall the event.

For many this is the beginning and end of it. It is a simple matter of obedience: "Jesus told me to be immersed; if he is to be my Lord, I must do what he says." And if that was all scripture said about the subject, that would settle it. We might still be curious to know why the Lord should want to test our submission by insisting that we are willing to appear dripping wet in front of gaping spectators! It would certainly be quite unlike him to order us to do anything that was not for our good, which would bless us as well as him.

Actually, it is a mistake to see baptism as something done by us for him. It is not just a human action. Other than agreeing to be baptized and arriving at an appropriate time and place, the main participant is passive rather than active. Baptism is not something we do to ourselves, another person does it to us. This is highly significant.

The biblical emphasis is not on what we do for the Lord, but on what he does for us. Baptism is more an act of deliverance than an act of obedience. Baptism actually works! Or rather, God works through baptism for our blessing.

So far we have only considered the practice – *how* we should be baptized. It is time to explore its purpose – *why* we should be baptized.

Over thirty passages in the New Testament testify to the wealth of meaning to be found in this simple act (you could profitably study one each day for a month). Two insights stand out clearly among the others. It is both a bath for dirty people and a burial for dead people. Obviously, total immersion is the only method that adequately expresses both aspects.

3

DIRTY PEOPLE NEED A BATH

Most of the water we use is for cleansing. We are forever washing ourselves and most things connected with us.

That is because dirt is our enemy. It can be disfiguring, damaging and even dangerous. It threatens us with disease and death.

Life is one long battle with dirt, as most children know! We spend an enormous amount of time, money and energy keeping it at bay. And it is noticeable that it is much easier to keep something clean if it starts clean.

Few people seem to be aware that there are two kinds of dirt. One is much easier to deal with than the other.

There is the dirt on the outside of us. Coal miners, garage mechanics and gardeners know all about this. It is fairly easily removed: a good scrub with hot water and soap is usually enough to shift it. Our skin helps us by renewing itself every few weeks, sloughing off the most obstinate stains.

There is another kind of dirt, on the inside of us, and this is a much bigger problem. Jesus referred to this when he said that nothing going into the mouth can make us unclean, but filthy things coming out of the heart do so (he listed greed, pride, envy, slander, lust and deceit; Mark 7:18–23).

There are even cases where people have so polluted themselves with dirty thoughts and feelings that they become possessed by an "unclean" spirit, one of the demonic agents of the devil seeking to destroy the image of God in us and rob us of our divine destiny.

We are talking about the difference between physical and moral dirt. Alas, we are usually far more concerned about the former than the latter. For Jesus and his Father, it is the other way around! His teaching about the dirty heart was prompted by the criticism that he allowed the disciples to eat food without first washing their hands.

At the very worst, physical dirt can cut this life short and bring it to an untimely end. Moral dirt, however, can bring an endless existence of misery in the next life (see my book, *The Road to Hell*). It is at the same time far more dangerous and far more difficult to remove. In fact, we can't do it for ourselves, as anyone who has really tried knows only too well. Many people give up quickly, accepting this moral dirt as a natural state ("after all, no one's perfect"). To live a pure life would be a supernatural achievement.

That's precisely what it is. The good news is that God sent his son Jesus to get us clean, and his Spirit to keep us clean. The "natural" dirty state is no longer inevitable; a supernaturally clean state is now possible. The very name Jesus was given because he would be the one, and the only one, who could *"save us from our sins"* (Matthew 1:21), cleaning up our lives from the inside out.

To make that possible, he first had to pay the penalty due to us, which he did on the cross, making both forgiveness and a restored relationship with God available to everybody. But how does all that become ours?

At the heart of the answer, although it is not the whole of it, lies baptism. From its first introduction, the intention of immersing people in water was to get rid of that inner dirt which the Bible calls *"sins"* (note the plural). John the Baptist said it was *"for the forgiveness of sins"* (Mark 1:4;

the Greek preposition is actually *eis*, meaning "into", and expresses both the purpose and result of doing something). So the effect of being plunged in the river Jordan was that sins were forgiven.

Of course, it was not quite as simple as that. The water wasn't magic and the washing wasn't automatic. The sins had first to be confessed – specifically and one by one. There is no such thing as a "general confession" or "sinner's prayer" in scripture – sins were always named; the Lord's prayer was intended as a guide rather than a formula).

Even before confession, there had to be repentance of the sins, including visible proof that they were no longer being practised (Luke 3:7–8). Without these preconditions, the water was not expected to cleanse the conscience (more of this in Chapter 8).

Though many other benefits were later added to full Christian baptism, the initial purpose of John always remained the basic one. On the day of Pentecost, Peter told his hearers: *"Repent and be baptized* [immersed], *every one of you ... for the forgiveness of sins"* (Acts 2:38). So far, this is word for word the preaching of John; however, Peter added two new ingredients – the name of Jesus Christ and the gift of the Holy Spirit (see Chapters 6 and 8).

Three days after he met Christ on the Damascus road, Saul of Tarsus (later Paul the apostle) was told by the elderly Ananias, *"And now what are you waiting for? Get up, be baptized* [immersed] *and wash your sins away, calling on his name"* (Acts 22:16). Later, Paul would write a letter to the church in Ephesus, reminding them that Jesus died to get the church cleaned up (*"to make her holy"*) and he did this by means of *"the washing with water through the word"* (Ephesians 5:26).

Yet another apostolic writer invites his reader to *"draw near to God with a sincere heart in full assurance of faith, having our hearts sprinkled to cleanse us from a guilty conscience* [that is, with the blood of Jesus] *and having our bodies washed with pure water"* (Hebrews 10:22). The same letter to the Hebrews lists baptism among the fundamental elements in the beginning of the Christian life (Hebrews 6:2).

It is, however, the fisherman Peter who makes this point most clearly. He points out that this immersion is not intended to remove dirt from the body, but is both a plea to God for a clean conscience and a pledge to keep it clean (1 Peter 3:21).

So the immersion in water is not expected to have any physical effect (though I know of a former "Hell's Angel" who lost a tattoo of the devil in his baptism). Nor is it expected to have any emotional effect (though it often does, from exciting exhilaration to profound peace). It is expected to have real moral and spiritual effects and these will be felt in the conscience.

It was my privilege to baptize the well-known singer, Cliff Richard. He describes the event in his autobiography (*Which One's Cliff?*, Hodder and Stoughton):

> David Pawson had referred earlier to baptism symbolizing a clean start and it was strange feeling of lightness that I felt as I clambered out of that little pool, all dripping and bedraggled. It wasn't an anti-climax or emptiness but an acute awareness that I really was free of all that spoilt and hindered and dragged me down. That's part of the fantastic miracle of what God does for a person.
>
> Christianity isn't about a life where hopefully and with super will-power, you slowly get cleaner and cleaner until finally you're there as some snow-white angel. The Christian actually starts clean. Once we accept for ourselves all that Jesus offers and start heading in his direction, we're washed, rinsed and hung up to dry right

there and then and, I tell you, to be able to hold your head up high, knowing that as far as God is concerned there's not a single blot on your copybook is something to get enthused about.

What could be better than a clean start for those who get themselves in a dirty mess? No wonder the Christian message is called the *"gospel"*! The word means simply "good news".

Even if this were the only benefit of baptism, it would make it infinitely worthwhile. But there's more, much more. It's not just a bath; it's also a burial.

4

DEAD PEOPLE NEED A BURIAL

Animals are rarely buried. Those that die in the wild are cleared up by scavengers, from vultures to maggots. The domesticated variety are either eaten or burned, depending on the manner of their death. Only the few kept so close to human beings that they are thought of as "one of the family" can expect to rest in a grave!

It is fitting to treat a human body differently, for it has belonged to someone bearing the image of God, unlike any animal. Human life is sacred. To treat humans as animals is sacrilege.

One purpose of burial is to veil the repulsive spectacle of a decaying corpse from prying eyes, so that the memory is untainted by this degrading process, which robs a person of dignity after they have died. Even before death, we can understand the biblical description: *"this body of our humiliation"*.

In some countries it has been the custom to expose executed criminals to the ultimate disgrace of public putrefaction by leaving the body on the gallows (a practice forbidden in Israel: Deuteronomy 21:23) or throwing it on the dump (which the Romans did). The body of Jesus might have suffered this fate (in the valley of garbage outside Jerusalem called Gehenna, which Jesus always used to picture hell), had Joseph of Arimathea not offered his own tomb.

It is right to give human beings the dignity of a proper funeral. After disasters at sea, on land or in the air, relatives are grievously frustrated if the bodies are beyond the reach of this last service that can be rendered to the departed. Even though the body is no longer part of that person, and never will be again, we still treat it with the respect we would give to the person to whom it once belonged. It is all that "remains" within the range of our care.

When Mary found the tomb of Jesus empty, she still thought of the body as "him" rather than "it" – and demanded that the "gardener" (whom she failed to recognise as the risen Jesus) disclose where "he" had been taken John 20:13–15).

This is probably why there is such an emphasis on the burial of Jesus. Paul includes it as one of the three most important facts of history on which our faith is based (1 Corinthians 15:4). The word "buried" has been included in every major creed (statement of faith) in the Christian church. It is not just there to inform us that Jesus had a proper funeral despite being executed as a criminal. It tells us that he really was dead. His body was properly disposed of. Nobody ever expected to see him again. The tomb was his final resting place. Only a supernatural intervention could change that.

But the miracle happened! God released him from the grave, even from the grave clothes. Life for Jesus, and indeed for everyone else, could never be the same again. Centuries before, God had promised that he would never leave the body of a truly holy person long enough in the grave to decompose (Psalm 16:10). Since decay really sets in on the fourth day (John 11:39), the "holy one" would need to be raised by the third. God kept his promise.

Buried – raised. That is also what happens in baptism.

It is the final break with the old life, which is now ended. That old life, centred on self, spoiled by sin and separated from God, carried within it the seeds of its own decay and death. Now it must be buried. The body that was used as an instrument of the world, the flesh and the devil must now be put out of sight, buried beneath the water.

Every baptism is a funeral service. That is why, of course, we don't baptize ourselves (corpses don't assist in their own interment). As one friend of mine says to all he baptizes, "It's your funeral; enjoy it!"

But Satan doesn't enjoy it; he hates it. He is angry whenever he loses one of his followers and knows that baptism represents their freedom from his control. Perhaps this is why he tries so hard to dissuade before and to tempt afterwards (he tried the latter with Jesus himself). It also explains why other religions often take baptism far more seriously than some Christians seem to do, regarding it as the ultimate act of treason against the faith in which they were brought up (there is sometimes a similar attitude towards those "christened" as babies who get baptized as believers). In some countries, baptism alone is sufficient to warrant the death penalty. We should not take it lightly, even though we may take it joyfully.

For we are not left in the watery grave. Otherwise, the churches would soon be very short of members! But being lifted out of the water has much more meaning than the practical need to start breathing again and avoid being drowned. Emerging is as meaningful as being submerged.

Baptism is a resurrection as well as a burial. It is a start as well as a finish, the beginning of a new clean life as well as the end of an old dirty one.

What happened to Jesus now happens to his followers. Everyone thought that his burial was the end of him. But it led to the resurrection and a whole new dimension of living.

It is the same for those who are baptized. If we have been buried with him, we are also raised with him – to new life and a new lifestyle (Romans 6:3-4).

I suppose that the simplest definition of a Christian is "someone who follows Jesus". But that could be interpreted (and misinterpreted) in a number of different ways. For some it has meant trying to live the way he lived ("What would Jesus do?") or trying to apply to themselves the principles of his moral teaching ("What would Jesus say?").

The New Testament concept of discipleship does not begin with either his life or his teaching, important though these are. The point of entry into the kingdom of heaven on earth is to be found in the death, burial and resurrection of Jesus – and of ourselves. To follow Jesus is to die to the old life of self and sin, to have it buried and to be raised to live a new life. This is precisely what takes place in baptism – and why it marks the beginning of the Christian way.

Yet when Paul develops this theme in his letter to the Romans, he takes it much further, with a rather surprising choice of words. Instead of saying that we are buried and raised *like* Christ, he says we are buried and raised *with* Christ – almost as if it is happening to him and to us at the same time!

Clearly, some deeper truth is coming through – and it is necessary to devote a whole chapter to it.

Note: For a fuller treatment of the connection between baptism and the risen life, see my booklet in this series, *Explaining the Resurrection*.

5

A CASE OF IDENTIFICATION

We use words to communicate thought to each other, but if words are to be understood, they must first be defined. The verb "identify" is used two different ways in the English language.

The simple meaning is "to recognise". Identifying a thing means recognising what it is and giving it a label. Identifying a person means recognising who they are and giving them a name.

The more subtle meaning is "to associate". It is usually limited to persons. To identify *with* someone (note the preposition) is to be so closely associated with them that you share their thoughts and feelings, their outlook and character and even find yourself treated in the same way. It is as if their identity has been transferred to you.

This experience of identification lies at the heart of the Christian gospel and our response to it.

Jesus Christ has identified himself with us

Jesus identified himself with us first, *by becoming human*. He always was the Son of God, equal to his Father in power and glory, sharing in the making and maintaining of our universe. But his Father wanted to "send" him to our planet to save us from ourselves – and he voluntarily "came", even though the mission would involve sharing the whole experience of being human.

So Jesus chose to be born (the only person who ever did), to become a foetus in a mother's womb, a baby at her breast, a boy at school and a carpenter in the workshop. Faced with temptation and suffering, he learned all over again how to obey his heavenly Father – by submitting to his earthly stepfather.

All this preparation for his main task took thirty years. It is almost impossible to imagine what patience and humility were required, knowing who he was (which he certainly did by the age of twelve; Luke 2:49). No one else has ever been willing, much less able, to make such a change in lifestyle.

What we do understand is that he became one of us, really one of us. We can dare to say that in Jesus, God identified himself with the human race. It is both a miracle and a mystery, but it is the truth.

So, for the first three decades of his life, the Son of God was regarded as just one human being among all the others. During this time he had many friends and no enemies (Luke 2:52). But all this was to change.

Jesus also identified with us *by being baptized*. His cousin John was horrified to see him standing in the line of people waiting to wash their sins away in the river. For Jesus it seemed both unnecessary and inappropriate. He had no sins to be confessed and forgiven. Jesus silenced John's objections by saying that for him baptism would be an act of righteousness, the right thing to do, something his Father had told him to do. This was confirmed by a loud voice from the sky (which many thought was just thunder), saying: *"This is my Son, whom I love; with him I am well pleased"* (Matthew 3:17).

In this simple act, Jesus was identifying with the sinful

people of Israel – standing with sinners, submitting to a bath with them, as if he was just as dirty as they were. Anyone watching could easily have assumed that he had secret sins to confess, of which they knew nothing. If they had thought that, he was unlikely to have enlightened them; the last thing to concern him was his reputation.

Baptism marked the beginning of Jesus' troubles. Launching him into his saving mission, it quickly led to conflict, first with the devil and his demons, and later with human foes, especially the rich, the religious and the respectable. Within months he had antagonised the Jewish authorities and soon his life was in danger. After escaping a number of attempted assassinations, he deliberately walked into a trap in Jerusalem. One of his closest companions betrayed him and he was condemned to a horrible death.

The third way that Jesus identified with us was *by being crucified*. This was to be his greatest act of identification with sinful human beings. Significantly, he referred to his death as a baptism: *"I have a baptism to undergo, and how distressed I am until it is completed!"* (Luke 12:50). Jerusalem is only fifteen miles from the Jordan, though it is fifteen hundred metres higher. It is as if Jesus saw his public ministry as a journey up the road between, from one baptism to another.

This time he would be submerged in suffering, plunged into excruciating pain. Falsely accused of the capital crimes of blasphemy and treason, he was treated as if he were the worst criminal on earth. Even more shocking, he was treated by God as if he was personally responsible for all the sins ever committed in the whole world. And he accepted this humiliation as if he deserved it.

At the time no one understood what was going on. At the height of the tragedy, even Jesus himself was bewildered (Mark 15:34), but this was a fleeting moment which reveals his genuine humanity. He had known before he died and would explain after he rose from the dead – that this was what he had come to do and was the greatest thing he would ever do for us all.

But what was he doing for us? Let his apostles tell us. Peter: *"He himself bore our sins in his body on the tree, so that we might die to sins and live for righteousness"* (1 Peter 2:24). Paul: *"God made him who had no sin to be sin for us"* (2 Corinthians 5:21). John: *"God ... loved us and sent his Son as an atoning sacrifice for our sins"* (1 John 4:10). In other words, he so identified himself with us that our sins became his and he paid for them with his life.

However, this is only half the story. His death, both instead of sinners and on their behalf, cannot benefit any of them until they apply it to themselves. Identification has two sides to it.

Christians identify themselves with him

Christians have become so intimately related to Jesus that what happened to him has, in a real sense, also happened to us. We not only believe that Jesus was crucified, buried and raised *for* us; we also believe that we have been crucified, buried and raised *with* him. His death is our death. His tomb is our grave. His resurrection is our new life.

Baptism is at the centre of this. It is supremely an act of identification with Jesus (read Romans 6 again, but this time verses 1–14). We are baptized *into* Christ. Just as we put on different (dry) clothes after being immersed, so we have *put on* and been *clothed with* Christ (Galatians 3:27).

We have taken on his identity. Our former identity is now secondary to this, whether we were Jewish or Gentile, male or female, enslaved or free. In Christ we are now new people, all children of God, and therefore heirs. As such we can now claim the blessing promised to one male descendant of Abraham (read the whole third chapter of Paul's letter to the Galatians). We shall even inherit the whole earth; everything is ours in Christ.

Everything includes trouble! Identification with Christ means sharing his sufferings. If his baptism led to conflict, ours is likely to do the same. If he was hated, so will we be. He was always totally honest about this, promising his disciples "big trouble" in this world, warning them that to follow him would mean carrying a cross every day, subject to hostility and humiliation. Don't share his baptism in the Jordan if you are not willing to share his *"baptism"* in Jerusalem (Mark 10:38).

If we are persecuted because of our identification with Jesus (and only for this), that is both a proof of our righteousness (2 Timothy 3:12) and a promise of our reward (Matthew 5:11–12). We shall share the glory that followed his sufferings and the joy that followed his shame (Luke 24:26; Hebrews 12:2). We will even count it an honour and privilege to be treated as badly as he was (Acts 5:41; Romans 5:3–4). If we endure, we shall reign with him (2 Timothy 2:12).

We can put all this a different way. If we have taken the identity of Christ, we now bear his name. This name is as much part of the baptism as the water.

6

WHAT'S IN A NAME?

John the Baptist saw immersion as an act of repentance, preceded by confession and leading to forgiveness. The change was moral and dealt with the sins of the past. So it looked backward and was essentially negative, a separation from what was wrong.

We have seen that this continued to be an essential aspect of Christian baptism. But after the death, burial and resurrection of Jesus much more meaning was added, giving the act a more positive and forward-looking significance – not just a removal of sins, but a relationship with the Saviour. The washing became a burial as well, with a resurrection to follow. Bonds of Satan are broken and bonds to Christ forged.

In fact it now meant so much more that those who had only had John's baptism were re-baptized. Though the outward form was identical (immersion in water), the words used were quite different. They were now baptized *"into the **name** of the Lord Jesus"* (Acts 19:5).

This name was on the lips of the person baptizing and the one being baptized. The former was using the name as his authority to perform the ceremony and the latter was encouraged to *"call on his name"* for the achieving of its purpose (Acts 22:16; cf. 2:21).

On the one hand, the early Christians realized that Jesus' name carried *authority*. The ascended Jesus is now in control of the entire universe (Matthew 28:18). Every baptism is done in obedience to his command and represents another addition to his kingdom.

On the other hand, it was now clear that Jesus' name conveyed *power*. In his name diseases were healed, demons were expelled and even death was reversed. The two central themes in the early Christian preaching were the kingdom of God and the name of Jesus (Acts 8:12). If you go through the book of Acts and underline the word *"name"*, you would be surprised at how often it appears.

This was not regarded as a magical incantation. The name would have been useless without the person and position behind it. What a help it is when a high official helps us to get what we need by sending us to the right place with the encouraging words: "Just mention my name." That is exactly what Jesus told us to do when we pray to God his Father (John 16:23–24).

To do anything in Jesus' name is to make it significant. Indeed, Christians are expected to do (and say) *everything* in his name (Colossians 3:17). That is because the baptized now bear his name. Their conduct and conversation will give him a good name or a bad name in the eyes of the world. It is a solemn responsibility.

Baptism is *"into"* the name of Jesus. We exchange our name for his, not another new one of our own (the practice of giving a new "Christian" name at baptism is a nice custom and may be helpful in making a fresh start, but it is not essential and could distract from the name of Jesus). It is *his* life we will be living, not ours (Galatians 2:20). So it is entirely appropriate that his name be both prominent and frequent during a baptism. There is no other name on earth that can save a sinner (Acts 4:12).

Before leaving this theme, it is necessary to consider an ambiguity in scripture that has led to some controversy.

WHAT'S IN A NAME?

Throughout the book of Acts, baptism is *"in"* or *"into"* the name of Jesus, Jesus Christ or the Lord Jesus – but always "Jesus". However, one verse, and only one, in the Gospels links a "Trinitarian" wording with baptism (Matthew 28:19; *"in the name of the Father and of the Son and of the Holy Spirit"*). Even in itself, this verse is a little confusing – since "name" is singular and neither "Father" nor "Son" is actually a name.

The debate over whether one name or three should be used has sometimes reached the point where each side declares the other invalid and demands re-baptism. Traditional churches have insisted on the threefold formula, while newer fellowships tend to have insisted on the name Jesus. It is important to distinguish between those who do not use the Trinitarian formula in baptism, and those who don't believe that God is three persons in one (the latter view is untrue to the New Testament and rightly regarded as heresy).

How do we explain the apparent discrepancy between what Jesus told the apostles to say and what they actually said? Did they forget, misunderstand, change or disobey what he had said? None of these possibilities fits in with what we know of them, particularly after they had been filled with the Spirit of truth, part of whose task was to safeguard their memory of Jesus' words (John 14:26). He must have done this for Matthew, as well as the other apostles!

The only conclusion that fits all the facts is that for the apostles the single name "Jesus" stood for all three persons of the Godhead – and invoked their presence and pleasure at the baptism. After all, the Father is the Father of Jesus, the name of the Son is Jesus, and the Spirit is the Spirit of Jesus. To know Jesus is to know the Father and the Spirit as well.

If the wording in Matthew (occurring only once) is used, the powerful name of Jesus may be totally omitted. If the wording in Acts (used many times) is used, the involvement of the Father and Spirit may be overlooked. There is far more warrant for using the name "Jesus", but my own practice has been to use both forms in a complementary way: "In the name of the Father, the Son and the Holy Spirit, we baptize you into Jesus Christ, into his death, burial and resurrection." In saying "we," I would be speaking on behalf of the whole church of Christ, but there would always be two of us doing the baptizing (so the focus would not be on the baptizer).

However, I suspect that the Lord is not quite so fussy or inflexible as ecclesiastical authorities tend to be. What I believe is of much more importance to him, and should be to us, is the spiritual state of the one being baptized.

What are the qualifications for baptism? When is a person ready for this once-in-a-lifetime event? When are they fit to bear his name?

7

PENITENT BELIEVERS ONLY

Without that remarkable man Abraham, I would not be writing this book and you would not be reading it. It is from him that we learn that faith means both trust and obedience.

At the age of eighty he left a comfortable house and lived in a tent for the rest of his life, pitching it in a land he had never seen before, which God promised to him and his descendants, though he and his wife were too old to have children. He believed that God would make him the father of many nations and a blessing to the whole earth. Such implicit faith pleases God as much as living a perfectly good life (Genesis 15:6).

Muslims, Jews and Christians all regard Abraham as their "father", though for quite different reasons. Arabs trace a physical ancestry back through Ishmael (whom God promised to make into a great nation with twelve rulers; Genesis 17:20). Jews trace their line back through Isaac; their claim to God's promises, including the "holy" land, rested on this heredity. Hence all males (females were not heirs) were circumcised on the eighth day as a seal of their heritage; this was simply a recognition that they were already qualified by birth (though if it were not done, they would be disqualified; Genesis 17:10–14).

Christians have become "sons of Abraham" by sharing his faith, not his flesh (Romans 4:16); they cannot be qualified by birth, so there is no Christian equivalent of circumcising male babies. Abraham's faith was truly amazing. He was willing to sacrifice his only legitimate son, Isaac, believing that God could raise him from the dead (Hebrews 11:19). He was content with his tent because he believed he would live one day in a marvellous city, designed and erected by God himself (Hebrews 11:10; we know it as the new Jerusalem – Revelation 21:10–27). He was thrilled when Jesus came to live among his descendants (John 8:56); for Abraham is still very much alive (Mark 12:26–27).

Those who believe as he did become his children (Galatians 3:7). So Gentiles can now become eligible to inherit the promise made to him (Galatians 3:14). But they do so through their faith, not their flesh. And this faith, in Abraham's descendant Christ, is expressed in baptism. Where Abraham was willing to leave his old land and go to a new one, in baptism we are saying goodbye to our old life and beginning a new one of trust and obedience.

Paul makes this link between Abraham and baptism in the passage already referred to (Galatians chapter 3, particularly verses 26–29: *"All of you who were baptized into Christ ... are Abraham's seed and heirs according to the promise"*). Because baptism is based on Abraham's faith and not his flesh, it requires our consent and cooperation; it represents a voluntary choice to trust and obey Christ. This is why it is so frequently linked with "conscience" in the New Testament (e.g. Hebrews 10:22; 1 Peter 3:21). Faith cannot be inherited. God has no grandsons.

Faith is therefore the basic requirement for anyone to be baptized. It is essential that faith is already being exercised before the baptism, if it is to be effective. However much faith there may be in the family from which the candidate comes or the church which they attend, nothing can take the place of their own personal reliance on Jesus.

So what is faith, this "saving faith" which, like Abraham's, will be *"credited to us as righteousness"* (Romans 4:20–22)?

It is based on fact, not feeling – the historical events of the death, burial and resurrection of Jesus, the Son of God. It is intensely personal, believing that he went through all this *"for us"* (Romans 4:23–25), which also means *"for me"* (Galatians 2:20). It is to believe that his death on the cross can take my sins away. It is to trust and obey him for the rest of my life.

I may have this faith in me, but it needs to come out if others are to know about it (including whoever decides to baptize me). I may have the right attitude to Jesus, but I can only prove that by appropriate actions. James, the brother of Jesus, is emphatic that faith without actions cannot save, it is as dead as a corpse (James 2:14–26). So what are these *"actions"*, *"deeds"* or *"works"* of faith?

There are two. Faith is to be expressed in word and exercised in deed. Faith is said and done (rather than thought and felt).

What's in the heart comes out of the mouth. If real faith is in the heart, it will emerge as words – which will be directed two ways. First, the true believer will ***"call on the name of the Lord"***, addressing him directly and appealing to him for help (Acts 2:21; "call" clearly suggests speaking aloud). Second, the true believer will ***"confess"*** before other people that Jesus is alive and is now his or her Lord (Romans 10:9–10). But faith needs to be practised as well as professed, if it is to be convincing (James 2:18–19).

Faith involves taking risks. It is a leap into the unknown, believing that the Lord will uphold and carry us. It is relying on him to guide and provide, rather than on other sources of security. It is to attempt things that are beyond our own resources and abilities. But all this is only to be done when he tells us. The line between faith and foolhardiness is narrow.

Rash ventures are tempting the Lord rather than trusting him (Matthew 4:7). Dependence cannot be separated from obedience.

How we have to exercise our faith will be different for each of us. The lives of the saints present us with an amazing variety; we must emulate their faith but not try to imitate their feats. We draw inspiration more than instruction from their exploits. The Lord may or may not tell us to build an ark or found an orphanage!

But there is one exercise of faith that is the same for all believers, regardless of age, class, race or sex. And it must begin before baptism, though it will continue afterwards. There can be no doubt that the Lord wants us to do it, because *"now he commands all people everywhere to repent"* (Acts 17:30). So what does *"repent"* mean?

Remember Abraham – who had to leave his old situation before he could go to the new one God had planned for him? He had to make a clean break with relationships and associations that would have held him back – even property. He had to say "No" to all that, in order to say "Yes" to God. Repentance is the negative side of faith.

John's baptism was *"of* [into] *repentance"* (Acts 19:4). It was the culmination of a clean break with a selfish, sinful way of life and a willingness to leave it all behind. A new start for the future involves a clean break with the past.

Repentance, like faith, is based on fact, not feeling. The fact is that all of us have defied God's authority, broken his laws, polluted his creation, hurt his children, spoiled his pleasure, ignored his appeals, refused his love, provoked his anger and deserved his judgment. Above all, our sins were responsible for the crucifixion of his Son, whom he had sent to save us.

Regret is what we feel when we realise what we have done to ourselves. Remorse is what we feel when we realise what we have done to others. Repentance is what we feel when we realise what we have done to God. But feelings vary from time to time and person to person. Repentance is not measured by the volume of tears, though if there are none it shows how sin has hardened our hearts.

Repentance, like faith, needs to be expressed in word and exercised in deed. It also is said and done.

Sins are to be confessed

It's quite easy, and pretty useless, to say: "I'm a sinner" (who isn't?). To say: "I have sinned", specifying how, is much harder, and much more healing. True confession is always particular – sins rather than sin in general. It is helpful to name sins aloud in the presence of the Lord, and in the presence of an understanding fellow believer.

Wrongs are to be righted

This is unlikely to happen unless specific sins have been mentioned. Only when they are faced one at a time is the Holy Spirit able to show us what needs to be done about them. In forgiving the past, God is not encouraging us to ignore it; he wants to give us grace to go back and put it right again. Removal of the divine penalty does not necessarily deal with the human consequences.

When Zacchaeus decided to repay with interest all those he had defrauded, Jesus said, "Today salvation has come to this house" (Luke 19:9). Repentance is very practical. John the Baptist gave some down-to-earth examples: giving away surplus clothing and food, being honest in business dealings and content with one's wages (Luke 3:7–14).

It is likely to be different for each person and focus on those things that have held them in slavery to sin and Satan. Some relationships will have to be broken off, others restored. Debts will have to be paid off, even crimes reported. Letters may have to be written, phone calls made, shelves and cupboards explored, things thrown away or destroyed (Acts 19:19).

Before John would baptize anyone, he demanded that such *"fruit in keeping with repentance"* be produced (Luke 3:8). Paul likewise told his hearers that they should *"turn to God and prove their repentance by their deeds"* (Acts 26:20).

Baptism is not for those who only *profess* to be penitent believers, but for those who can *prove* that they are. Anyone asking for baptism should be willing to demonstrate that they are ready; anyone asked to baptize should require it.

Repentance and faith can only be proved if they are already being practised. Both must begin before baptism if it is not to be an empty ritual, achieving nothing. Both must continue after baptism, for repentance and faith are a way of life. A good finish is as important as a good start. To ensure that, a believer needs two baptisms, one in water and one in Spirit.

Note: for fuller information on this subject, see these booklets: *Explaining Repentance* by Ed Roebert, and *Explaining Faith* by Colin Urquhart.

8

WATER AND SPIRIT

Many expect too little from their baptism. Some expect too much.

The problem is staying clean. The first sin after baptism can be traumatic. Have I undone it? Didn't it work? Has there been no change? Didn't I repent or believe enough? Such inner doubts can lead to disappointment, disillusion and even despair.

A few contemplate asking for another baptism, to get clean again. If that line is pursued, baptism could become a regular habit! This has sometimes caught on (among Coptic Christians in Ethiopia, for example). Centuries ago, some postponed their baptism until they were on their death-beds, to minimise the risk of rendering it invalid by subsequent sin. All these distortions are dealt with by Jesus' correction of Peter's thinking when, having first refused to have his feet washed, he then demanded that he be washed all over: *"Those who have had a bath need only to wash their feet; their whole body is clean"* (John 13:10).

We live in a dirty world and we are likely to pick up dirt as we walk through it. But there is a remedy for this: if we go on confessing our sins, he goes on forgiving us and the blood of Jesus goes on cleansing us (1 John 1:7–9). But surely we're not meant to go on like this? Why doesn't our baptism break this vicious circle and help us to keep clean?

Part of the answer is that we need to keep applying our baptism. Since we have been buried, we must constantly *"reckon"* or *"count"* ourselves *"dead"* (Romans 6:11). That's what our baptism added up to. It is only because we retain the old body's habits and the old brain's memories that we are deluded into thinking the old person is still alive. But we need to (and can) re-programme our minds. Recalling our baptism is one way of doing this. We can call Satan's bluff by reminding him and ourselves about the funeral!

But this is only part of the answer. Immersion in water was never intended to be the full or final solution to the problem of sin. It was designed to deal with past sins, not future sins; to get us clean, not keep us clean.

John the Baptist was very much aware of the limitations of his ministry (he never performed any miracles, for example) and the scope of his water baptism. He knew how easily sins return to spoil a clean life. He felt he was just preparing the way for someone else to do two more things for the people, which would make all the difference to their battle with temptation. They needed to have their sins taken away, and not just forgiven; and they needed to be baptized in the Holy Spirit. This would be the dual mission of the coming King (John 1:29, 33).

Was he surprised when God used a dove to identify his cousin Jesus as the one to do both? Or had his mother Elizabeth told him that Mary was the mother of the Messiah? Perhaps what was new was the realisation that there were to be two baptisms and two baptizers (both John and Jesus are called baptists, baptizers, immersers, dippers). One baptism was in water, which anyone could do; the other was in the Holy Spirit, which only Jesus could do.

The phrase *"baptized in the Holy Spirit"* occurs in all four Gospels, in the book of Acts and in the epistles (Matthew

3:11; Mark 1:8; Luke 3:16; John 1:33; Acts 1:5, 11:16; 1 Corinthians 12:13).

Other phrases are used synonymously to describe the same event – *"filled"* with the Holy Spirit, *"receiving"* the Holy Spirit, *"sealed"* with the Holy Spirit, *"anointed"* with the Holy Spirit. More dramatic descriptions speak about the Spirit *"coming upon"* people, *"falling on"* them or being *"poured out"* on them. The wide vocabulary indicates a rich experience.

There is clearly a close link between the two baptisms. They usually happen very close together, though never simultaneously. On most occasions, baptism in the Spirit happens at the time of baptism in water, as was the case with Jesus himself (Matthew 3:16). The early church took his experience as the usual pattern to be expected.

Sometimes it happened much later (Acts 8:16) and once just before (Acts 10:46; perhaps this was because the Jew Peter would never have baptized Gentiles until he saw this incontrovertible evidence that God had accepted them).

After preaching his first-ever sermon, Peter told his hearers if each one of them would repent and be baptized, they would not only be forgiven but would also receive the same gift of the Spirit he and his friends had just received (Acts 2:38). When Paul met some disciples who had not "received" the Holy Spirit, his very next question was about their baptism in water, showing how closely the two were connected in his own thinking. Learning that they had only been through John's baptism of repentance, he led them to full faith in Jesus, and baptized them into Jesus' name in water. And afterwards Jesus baptized them in the Spirit, in response to Paul's prayer for them (Acts 19:1–6).

So the two baptisms belong together. Both are necessary, both are freely available and both should be sought. To be cleaned up and then merely left empty is not only disappointing, it is positively dangerous. Jesus told a parable about seven unclean spirits moving into a clean but vacant house where only one spirit had lived before (Matthew 12:43–45).

There are two verses in the New Testament which link the two baptisms together in quite a profound way. One is well known, the other hardly noticed. They are in different books but have the same chapter and verse numbers! Both are concerned with being *"born again"* or regeneration.

In the first, Jesus is explaining to the Jewish theologian Nicodemus that life in the Kingdom of God begins with a second birth, which he describes as being *"born* [out] *of water and the Spirit"*, which implies being first put into water and the Spirit (John 3:5). One verb and preposition with two nouns indicates both the similarity and the difference between the two, as well as the close connection between them.

In the second, Paul is instructing Titus to remind those he teaches that they were not saved *by* their good deeds, but *because* of God's mercy and *through* the *"washing of rebirth"* (which Calvin, among many other scholars, took as a reference to baptism) and *"renewal by the Holy Spirit whom he **poured out** on us generously"* (Titus 3:5).

It is not hard to identify water baptism: both participant and spectators know exactly when that happens. There should be the same certainty about Spirit baptism, though many have considerable doubt about this.

Perhaps that is due to a widespread notion in the contemporary church that baptism in the Spirit is automatic and usually unconscious. Those holding this view then argue about whether it happens during the dispensing of a sacrament, either christening or confirmation (the "Catholic" view) or when a conversion takes place (the "Evangelical" view). The weakness in this approach becomes apparent in the extreme reluctance to use biblical terminology to describe what has happened, for it would then be quite inappropriate to say "baptized," "immersed," "poured out" or "fallen upon."

The truth is that in the New Testament, Spirit baptism was both audible and visible. Something clearly happened, so that both participants and spectators knew *whether* and *when* it did. One biblical scholar says it was "as definite as catching influenza." The reader may easily check this out (see, for example, Acts 8:16–18 and 19:2–6; Galatians 3:2).

So what is the outward evidence that Spirit baptism has taken place? In the case of Jesus a "dove" alighted on his head; on the day of Pentecost, flames appeared. But both signs were unique to these special occasions and were not repeated. What happened on all other occasions was that people were so filled with the Holy Spirit that they overflowed in speech.

On many occasions they poured out words in a language they had never spoken before. This is not surprising since it was God who was originally responsible for all the different languages and he speaks them all (Genesis 11:9). At other times, they burst into spontaneous praise or prophecy in their own language (Acts 10:46 and 19:6). Even bystanders knew something was going on, though they did not always reach the right conclusion (Acts 2:13–15) or make the right response (Acts 8:18–19).

Though this verbal overflow was spontaneous, it was not forced on anyone. The Holy Spirit treats us as persons, not puppets. He doesn't make us do anything we are unwilling to do. We can suppress his moving within us and refuse to let it out. Fears and inhibitions can delay Spirit baptism as well as water baptism. We must want both the in-filling and the out-pouring.

When we want something badly enough, we go on asking

for it. So pray for it to happen, as Jesus seems to have done immediately after his immersion in water (Luke 3:21). We needn't fear that God would allow us to receive anything harmful: *"If you, then, though you are evil, know how to give good gifts to your children, how much more will your Father in heaven give the Holy Spirit to those who ask* [or, *go on asking*] him" (Luke 11:13).

Others can pray for you to receive the Holy Spirit. They can *"lift up holy hands in prayer"* (1 Timothy 2:8) or *"lay* [place] *hands"* on you, which is a very meaningful and effective form of prayer, clearly appropriate in this connection (Acts 8:17–18; 19:6). One scripture verse suggests that this was a common practice in the early church (Hebrews 6:2).

Soaked in water and saturated in the Spirit – that is a description of every member of the apostolic church in the New Testament. That is what qualified them to be members. That is what actually made them members.

Note: Though Spirit baptism is not really the subject of this book, it is so closely linked to water baptism that it was impossible to ignore it. For fuller information, we recommend *Explaining the Holy Spirit* by Dr. Bob Gordon.

9

THE CHURCH DOOR

There is a widespread assumption that every baptism ought to be public. Many see it as a testimony to others that one now belongs to Jesus Christ. They find a precedent in Timothy's *"good confession in the presence of many witnesses"* (1 Timothy 6:12), though it does not specifically mention baptism.

The spectacle of immersion certainly makes an impact. Unbelievers are challenged about their willingness (or unwillingness) to do the same – and therefore to question their relationship with the Lord. Believers are reminded of their own baptism, remembering what it meant, and still means, to them. Often they wish they could get into the water again (a similar reaction to witnessing a wedding)!

For the participants, baptism presents a wonderful opportunity to "go public" with their faith. They show that they are unashamed to be associated with Jesus, whatever the cost or consequences. It is a reminder of the opposite – that if we disown him, he will disown us (Mark 8:38; 2 Timothy 2:11–13).

Having said all this, there are real difficulties in regarding baptism simply as a public testimony. For one thing, the immersion in water loses its point. Why does the "witness" have to be wet? Is it a device to test our courage by public humiliation? That seems out of character with our Lord.

More importantly, there is no direction in the New Testament, either explicit or implicit, that baptism should be administered in public. On a number of occasions, it is doubtful if there were many, or even any, spectators (Acts 8:36–38, 9:18 and 16:33). Nor is there any evidence that the church had to be gathered for the occasion, though no doubt they did when they could – and there are obvious reasons why this is desirable, even though it is not essential.

Only two people are really necessary – the one baptizing and the one baptized. And it can be done anywhere there is sufficient water (John 3:23). Provided it is done to a penitent believer in the name of Jesus, the baptism is fully valid.

For baptism is essentially an individual matter. Notice how Peter emphasised this in his first sermon: *"Repent and be baptized, **every** [or, each] **one** of you ..."* (Acts 2:38). The gospel is for *"whoever is believing"* (John 3:16). Whole households were only baptized when every member (including all relatives and slaves) responded to the preaching in faith (Acts 16:33–34, 18:8).

Paradoxically, though it may be done privately, baptism cannot be a private matter! To put it another way, although it is applied to the individual, it is the end of individualism. We may not be baptized *in* a community, but we are baptized *into* a community. This may not be immediately obvious, so we shall retrace our steps to an earlier part of the explanation (Chapter 5). When we are baptized into Christ and take his name, our own identity is merged with his. We are united with him and "become one" with him. We are also united with all the others who have been baptized into Christ, identified and united with him. We are no longer separate individuals with differences of race, sex or class dividing us from each other. We are now *"all one in Christ Jesus"*

(Galatians 3:28; note the context of baptism). Jesus has united Jew and Gentile in *"one new humanity"* (Ephesians 2:15).

We can approach this truth from another angle. When we are baptized into Christ, we are joined to his whole being. It is impossible to be united to the "head" in heaven without becoming part of his "body" on earth.

This unity between baptized believers is an accomplished fact. It exists from the moment we identify with Christ. As Paul says: *"There is one body and one Spirit – just as you were called to one hope when you were called – one Lord, one faith, one baptism; one God and Father of all, who is over all and through all and in all"* (Ephesians 4:4–6). Note the Trinitarian character of this unity, the centrality of faith and baptism, in that order, and above all, the comprehensive nature and purpose of God.

But this unity needs to be *"kept"* (Ephesians 4:3) - which implies the danger that it can be lost. It has to be expressed and exhibited, which requires much effort on our part. This is just another example of our need to work out the salvation that God has worked in (Philippians 2:12–13). The place to do this first is in the local church.

Jesus used the word "church" in two ways. When he said, *"I will build my church"* (Matthew 16:18), he was clearly referring to the universal company of all his disciples, now numbering millions, both on earth and in heaven. Its unity consists in having one divine head, not one human headquarters! But when he said, *"Tell it to the church"* (Matthew 18:17), he was clearly referring to a local community that could be addressed by one of its members.

When we are baptized into Christ, we become members of the universal church automatically, without any choice in the matter or any action on our part. However, both are needed to become members of a local church, especially when there is more than one within easy reach of where we live or work.

For new Christians it is usually wise to join that local church through which they were brought to belief in, and baptism into, Christ. If this is impossible, they should look for the one that is nearest to their physical location and their spiritual understanding. In cases of difficulty, Jesus, the head of the church is always available for consultation - pray about it! He wants to see every "new-born baby" properly cared for in a family of loving brothers and sisters.

Of course, the family must be willing to undertake this responsibility. Nobody should be baptized without making sure that they will be looked after, either within that church or another. New converts should be received into membership without any further qualifications than having repented of their sins towards God, believed in Jesus Christ as Saviour and Lord, been baptized in water and received the Holy Spirit. These are the four steps up to the front door of the church and should be sufficient qualification for membership; no more (and no less) should be expected at that stage.

Alas, many churches add their own conditions and make it much harder to be part of the local church than the universal church! Of course there are many more steps to be taken, but the staircase belongs inside the house, not outside. Children belong to a family before they have learned how to behave in it.

The transfer of mature disciples from one local church to another is quite a different ministry. It is then appropriate to expect them to demonstrate consistency with biblical standards of belief and behaviour, together with acceptance of discipline under the recognised leaders.

So, while baptism does not of itself make anyone a member of a local church, it should lead on to that as soon as possible. To claim to belong to the church of Christ while standing aloof from involvement in a local church would be as incongruous as wanting to be a soldier without joining a regiment, or a sailor without joining a ship.

There is something more to be said about church membership. It is not the same as membership of a club or society. That involves getting one's name on the books, paying subscriptions, attending meetings, electing officers and generally supporting its objectives and activities.

The church is not so much a body of persons as a body belonging to a Person. Like a human body, it has limbs and organs which must function in a coordinated way or the whole body becomes sick. If part is cut off, the body is "dismembered." The less visible functions are often the most important. None can do without the others.

All this applies to the church (read 1 Corinthians 12). Just what role or function each member has is not their choice or that of the other members. That is decided by the three persons of the Godhead (1 Corinthians 12:4–6), though it is discovered by the members.

The differing functions are supernatural abilities, gifts of grace (in Greek they are called *charismata*, from which we get the adjective "charismatic"). We are allowed, even commanded, to *"eagerly desire"* the best gifts (1 Corinthians 14:1), but we cannot choose them. And we are not to covet them for status, but for service. How and when do these gifts start functioning?

Water baptism may introduce us to the body of Christ, but it is Spirit baptism that releases our gifting. *"For we were all baptized by one Spirit into one body ... and were all given the one Spirit to drink"* (1 Corinthians 12:13; note the repetition of *"one"* and that the tense of the verbs refers to a once-for-all event). This verse is central to a whole chapter about spiritual gifts, which together build up ("edify", the verb of the noun "edifice") the body of Christ.

The Spirit produces fruit as well as gifts, character as well as capability. Fruit without gifts can limit the body, but gifts without fruit can damage it. This fruit (singular) has at least nine flavours (Galatians 5:22–23). Together they duplicate the character of Christ himself, especially his greatest attribute of love.

So from the corporate as well as the individual angle, both baptisms are necessary and belong together. Both the person and the people of Christ need to be separated from a sinful past (by baptism in water) and supplied with a sanctifying power (by baptism in Holy Spirit). In both the Old and the New Testaments, God says to us: *"Be holy, because I am holy"* (Leviticus 19:2; 1 Peter 1:16). For that we shall need every bit of help he offers us.

You now know more than enough about water baptism to decide both what to think and what to do about it. You could close the book at this point and not really miss any vital information.

However, not all Christians or all churches would agree with everything I have said so far. Sadly, baptism has been a subject of considerable controversy down the centuries and there are some deep differences about its meaning and practice – as you will soon discover, if you have not already done so. There is something you can do about this and something I can do about it.

Should you find yourself embroiled in discussion, go through this book again, checking everything against what the Bible says. If you cannot find my teaching within its pages, then forget it. If you do find it there, accept it from the Lord rather than from me.

For my part, I am adding three more chapters to help you think through some of the issues which have been debated and even been divisive. Inevitably, I will be sharing my own conclusions. It is impossible to be neutral or "objective" about something that calls for personal commitment rather than detached opinion. I have honestly considered all other viewpoints but always tried to let scripture speak for itself and decide for me.

There are three questions I will do my best to discuss with you:

- Isn't baptism just a symbol? (Chapter 10)
- Must we be baptized to be saved? (Chapter 11)
- Should babies be baptized? (Chapter 12)

10

SYMBOL OR SACRAMENT?

Symbols are pictures which point beyond themselves to something else - but do no more than that. Road signs make much use of them, warning about sharp bends, railway crossings or obstructions ahead. Then there are symbolic actions, such as the international gesture for hitchhiking, with the pointing thumb.

Many think that baptism is no more than a symbol, a re-enacted ritual that says a lot, but actually does nothing. It represents a great deal, but reproduces nothing. It only looks like a bath and a burial, but in neither case is it the real thing. It reminds us of certain realities in the Christian experience, but does not bring these about. It is simply a dramatic demonstration.

There are three important consequences following from this understanding.

First, the symbol becomes separated in time from the reality to which it corresponds. When a believer is baptized, this portrays an event which it is believed has already happened in the spiritual realm. When a baby is baptized, the time warp is even greater since this portrays an event which may not take place for many years to come.

Second, the symbol becomes quite secondary to the reality it represents – and therefore not really necessary. The really essential part of baptism becomes the "spiritual" bath and burial, not the outward act. Baptism is then in danger of becoming an optional extra, however helpful and desirable it may appear to be.

Third, the emphasis shifts from what the Lord does for us in baptism to what we do for him. It is only necessary as an act of obedience to him (or of testimony to others). It does something for God, but nothing for us. It is a human, rather than a divine, act.

However, this is very different from the way the New Testament speaks. The language about baptism is instrumental rather than symbolic. It is *for* the forgiveness of sins, it *is* a washing of rebirth and renewal, it *is* a burial and resurrection with Christ (Acts 2:38; Titus 3:5; Romans 6:3–4). Saul, later Paul, was told to delay his baptism no longer but get into the water and have his sins washed away (Acts 22:16).

This is the language of divine action, not human acting. The emphasis is on what baptism does - or rather, what the Lord does in baptism. The effects of baptism are expected at the time of baptism. Symbol and reality are simultaneous, because the one communicates the other. The visible enactment does not point to a past or future event; it is a present event, taking place before the eyes of the beholder.

This is what is meant by calling it a "sacrament." The word originally meant an oath of allegiance (taken by a Roman soldier to his Emperor, called the "sacramentum"); but in the church it is used of those events which mediate the grace of God. One well-known definition is: "an outward and visible sign of an inward and visible grace". However, even this definition could be misunderstood as being only symbolic. So let us be more specific: a sacrament is "a physical action with a spiritual effect."

Such a definition would offend many; they would not consider it acceptable or even possible in the real world in which we live. Why do they find it such a difficult idea? Because their minds have been too deeply influenced by ancient philosophy and modern science.

Western education and culture have been much more influenced by Greek ideas than Hebrew thinking. A major feature of the Greek world view was a division of the spiritual from the physical, the sacred from the secular, the eternal from the temporal. Plato found the spiritual world more real, Aristotle the physical (he was the first to teach evolution); but both divided reality into these two parts. Man's "immortal soul" must be saved from the body, a process completed by death.

Modern science has tended to make the same sharp distinction (often dismissing the spiritual as unreal). Nature is regarded as a closed system, controlling itself independently of any external power, according to its own "laws" (a view which is beginning to break down as more random chaos is discovered). Even if it was not self-created, it is certainly self-controlled.

Both the ancient and modern versions of this separation of the physical and the spiritual rule out any interaction between the two. The spiritual cannot affect the physical, which rules out miracles. The physical cannot affect the spiritual, which rules out sacraments.

Hebrew thinking is quite different. God is both Creator and controller of the universe. Since he is Spirit, but created matter, both are real and closely inter-related. The physical world is to be affirmed and enjoyed (marriage is as honourable as celibacy). Man's future hope is in the resurrection of the body, not the immortality of the soul.

The whole Bible rests on this Hebrew understanding of physical/spiritual interaction. Among other things it means that God can use physical objects and actions to achieve spiritual results. Scripture is full of such "sacramental" examples, beginning with the two trees in the Garden of Eden, which conveyed life and death. Moses could wave a rod over the Red Sea and God parted it. Naaman could bathe in the Jordan and his leprosy was healed.

This link between the natural and the supernatural has its dangers. To worship an idol (though it is only a lump of wood, metal or stone) can lead to contact with the personal forces of evil haunting our world. That is why God's people Israel were forbidden to wear charms, use divining rods or practice mediumistic techniques.

Though the New Testament is written in the Greek language, it is still Hebrew in thought; all its authors were Jewish (except the doctor Luke, all of whose material was Jewish). Laying hands on the sick can release divine healing. Even spittle mixed with clay can bring sight to the blind.

When the early Christians ate bread and drank wine, they were not just recalling Christ's past sacrifice on the cross; they were enjoying present participation ("communion") in his body and blood (1 Corinthians 10:16; note the following warning against eating meat offered to idols and the reference to baptism earlier in the chapter). If the bread and wine were not taken in the right manner, partakers could be judged by the Lord, suffering sickness and even death (1 Corinthians 11:27–32).

Why, then, should we think it strange that baptism will achieve what it symbolizes, convey what it represents, dispense what it depicts? That is thoroughly consistent with the outlook of the whole Bible. God can and does control all that he has made. He communicates with us by means of what he has made. He can convey his grace and power to us through anything he has made.

This is not magic, which seeks to manipulate supernatural forces for our purposes, whether supposedly good (white magic) or evil (black magic). This is God choosing both the end and the means for our salvation. We are not trying to get him to do something he doesn't want to do. He loves to give his children a new, clean start in life - and this is the way he has chosen to do that for us. That is his freedom of choice; our freedom is limited to accepting his offer or refusing it.

When baptism is explained like this, two objections are made, usually by evangelical Christians.

First, isn't this to fall into the error of "baptismal regeneration"? This phrase is usually taken to mean that baptism by itself is all that is needed to be "born again" into the kingdom of God and delivered from a lost eternity. Doesn't this encourage a false sense of security in those who have received the sacrament but have no personal faith in Christ (perhaps the majority of the population in some European countries)?

This distortion has been fostered wherever babies are baptized – for in their case baptism is administered by itself. Yet the liturgy used often states, or at least implies, that the baby has been "born again" and "saved". Inevitably, the impression is left that nothing more is needed (another cogent reason for questioning the whole practice of infant baptism).

In the New Testament, baptism is never "by itself". It is always preceded by repentance and faith and completed by the gift of the Spirit. It is only part of a complex of initiation – and is only believed to "work" in this context. Only then can it be called *"the washing of rebirth and renewal"* (Titus 3:5).

Second, doesn't this make baptism essential to salvation? And what does that mean for unbaptized believers? For example, if baptism is for the forgiveness of sins, does that mean that those who are not baptized are not forgiven? This question deserves a chapter of its own.

11

BAPTISM SAVES YOU NOW

"Must I be baptized to be saved?"

Like many questions, this one is loaded with assumptions and must be very carefully analysed (this is why Jesus often answered a question by asking one).

The word "must" may reflect a reluctance to accept God's way of doing things rather than eagerness to follow it. It's as if we want to know the bare minimum that would qualify, instead of wanting all that God has for us. To try and get around his requirements reveals a desire to make our own conditions, which is the essence of sin and needs to be included in our repentance.

But it is the word "saved" that needs to be looked at in depth.

If the questioner is asked: "Saved from what?" the inevitable reply is "Hell." The concern is with the next world rather than this, life after death rather than before. This is the legacy of a simplistic evangelism that presents the gospel as an insurance policy for the afterlife.

The Son of God came to earth to save us from our sins, which is precisely why he was called Jesus (Matthew 1:21). He is the Lamb of God who has come to take away the sin of the world (John 1:29), to break their power over us as well as to bear their penalty for us, to clean up our lives in this world and get us ready for life in heaven.

So the question must be rephrased: "Need I be baptized to be saved from my sins in this world?" To put it even more clearly: "Can I begin and continue to live a clean life without baptism?" Once we have realized that salvation means "salvaged from sins" rather than "safe from hell," both the question and the answer have quite a different tone about them.

Too many want to be happy in the next life rather than holy in this one. They want to be safe rather than saved. They are usually looking for an instant, even instantaneous, salvation that can be guaranteed as soon and as quickly as possible.

However, salvation is a process. It takes time, a lifetime. It begins with justification (freedom from the penalty of sin), continues with sanctification (freedom from the power of sin) and is completed in glorification (freedom from the presence of sin). In the New Testament the verb "to save" is used in past, present and future tenses - we *have been* saved, we *are being* saved and we *will be* saved.

Jesus came the first time to begin the process by removing the barrier of sin between us and God and reconciling us to him. He will *"appear a second time, not to bear sin, but to bring salvation to those who are waiting for him"* (Hebrews 9:28).

Salvation is a journey, a "pilgrim's progress." The first name for Christianity was *"the Way"* (Acts 18:25–26; 19:9, 23; 22:4; 24:22); that was also one of the titles Jesus gave himself (John 14:6). We can be sure we are "on the way", though we will not be safe until we arrive at our destination. Those who *"stand firm to the end will be saved"* (Matthew 24:13), who stay in Christ the *"true vine"* (John 15:5–6), who continue in God's kindness (Romans 11:22), who finish the race (2 Timothy 4:7), running with perseverance (Hebrews 12:1), making their calling and election sure (2 Peter 1:10), keeping themselves in God's love (Jude 21) and overcoming all temptations to give up (Revelation 3:5).

To get there will require all the help we can get from the Lord. To question whether anything he tells us to do is really necessary betrays a self-confidence that is taking a serious risk and an impudence which challenges divine wisdom.

"Must I be baptized to be saved?" The apostles would have been astonished by the question, which apparently never occurred to them or anyone else - or the answer would be in the Bible. Instead, we find everywhere the assumption that baptism is an essential step "on the way". To them an unbaptized disciple would have been a contradiction in terms.

There is not a single case of anyone being "saved" without baptism *after* the first Easter and Pentecost. There were, of course, some *before* that. Zacchaeus is one and the dying thief is another. Some simply couldn't be baptized in water (the thief nailed to the cross is only a precedent for those in similar circumstances!). None could be baptized in Holy Spirit, because he was not yet given (John 7:39). But they all did as much as they could; their repentance and faith sufficed.

The same is true for all who were saved in the Old Testament. Their outstanding faith, based on far less than ours, is an example and challenge to us (read Hebrews 11). They also did what they could.

But it is a scriptural principle that from those who are given more, more will be required (Luke 12:48). Once Christ had done all that was necessary for our salvation, we have to do all that is necessary to appropriate that salvation and make it our own.

Some protest that this introduces the "heresy" of salvation by works, by our efforts rather than by his grace. But in telling us that we need to repent (and prove that by our deeds), that we need to believe (and show that in our actions) and that we need to be baptized (in water and Spirit), the apostles were not telling us that we could save ourselves, much less earn our salvation by our good deeds. They were telling us that this is the way to be *"saved by grace"*.

When Peter exhorted his hearers to *"be saved from this corrupt generation"* (Acts 2:40; the translation *"save yourselves"* is inaccurate and misleading), he told them they must "repent and be baptized" (Acts 2:38). A drowning man who grabs and holds onto a lifeline thrown to him is under no illusion that he has saved himself!

The apostles never hesitated to ascribe saving effects from baptism. The title of this chapter ("Baptism saves you now") comes from the pen of Peter (1 Peter 3:21). Baptism brings forgiveness of sins (Acts 2:38), washing them away (Acts 22:16). Baptism frees from sin (Romans 6:4–7), cleanses the church (Ephesians 5:26), buries and raises with Christ (Colossians 2:12) and enables us to draw near to God (Hebrews 10:22). It is the bath of regeneration, the washing of rebirth (Titus 3:5).

In using such strong language about baptism, the apostles were following their Master's example. It was he who said: *"Whoever believes and is baptized will be saved"* (Mark 16:16; he adds that not believing is enough to be condemned - implying that baptism without faith cannot save). It was Jesus who told Nicodemus about being *"born again out of water and the Spirit"* (John 3:5; why do most preachers ignore the *"water"* here, though most scholars refer it to baptism, as in 3:22–23 and 4:1–2?).

We are now ready to answer the question with which we began: "Must I be baptized to be saved?" The answer is: "You shouldn't even be asking the question!" It is the wrong question for anyone who wants to become a disciple of Jesus and follow him. Even Jesus himself was baptized, *"to fulfil all righteousness"* (Matthew 3:15). The gospel is not just to be "received"; it is to be *"obeyed"* (Acts 16:32–33,

2 Thessalonians 1:8).

It is ridiculous to want to be saved without being willing to accept the way that Jesus has chosen to save us. That's like asking a surgeon to operate on us without using the knife or asking a dentist to fill a tooth without using the drill! We come to Christ his way or not at all. It was he who decided that every disciple should be baptized (Matthew 28:19).

Nor is it necessary to understand all that it means beforehand. Most of the New Testament teaching about its significance is given in retrospect. How many really appreciate the full implications of their marriage vows at the time of the wedding? The ceremony will mean more and more as time passes, but will never need to be repeated.

So *"what are you waiting for? Get up and be baptized and have your sins washed away, calling on his name"* (Acts 22:16)! You won't then have arrived at your destination, but you'll have set off in the right direction. All you've got to do now is keep going and you'll get there. When you do, you'll recall that your journey to the promised land began by going through the water. It has always been so for God's people.

12

BABY OR BELIEVER?

About half the professing Christians in the world today were "baptized" in the first few weeks of life, without their knowledge or consent. This proportion is now steadily declining, but it has been the general practice of the church for a major part of its history.

When did it begin? More importantly, why did it begin and why did it continue for so long?

Most biblical scholars are prepared to admit that infant baptism is nowhere to be found in the New Testament. However, some claim to find indirect references.

Six have been particularly mentioned:

1. Jesus blessed little children (Mark 10:13–16). But they were not new-born babies and he didn't baptize them.
2. Peter said: *"the promise is to you and your children"* (Acts 2:39). But the promise was Spirit baptism, not water baptism, and was also for "all who are far off," indeed all whom the Lord calls and who respond with repentance.
3. Paul baptized whole households, which must have included babies (e.g. Acts 16:33-34). But *"households"* included all relatives and servants as well and it specifically stated that the word was spoken to everyone in the household and that all received and believed it (see also Acts 18:8).
4. Paul said that in a mixed marriage the unbelieving

partner is *"sanctified"* and that the children are *"holy"* (1 Corinthians 7:14). But there is no mention of baptizing the children, much less the unbelieving parent.

5. Paul mentions circumcision and baptism together in one passage (Colossians 2:11–12). But this is the only such mention and refers to a "spiritual" circumcision (not *"done by human hands"*, not the physical rite - meaning to put off the sinful nature, as Christ died to sin on the cross. It is strange that in all Paul's vehement arguments against physical circumcision (in Acts 15 and the whole letter to the Galatians), he never once suggested that it was obsolete because baptism had taken its place.

6. Paul told children to *"obey* [their] *parents in the Lord"* (Ephesians 6:1). But the children are old enough to be addressed as responsible and they are not said to be *"in the Lord"* because of their birth or baptism as a baby (actually, the phrase *"in the Lord"* could refer to the parents rather than the children).

To these passages some add the general observation that in a "missionary" (i.e. pioneer) situation, the first generation is bound to consist of adult converts to the faith; only in the second generation will there be babies to baptize. But surely from the very beginning there would be parents with newly-born offspring (Jewish proselyte baptism immersed parents and children together, so why is there no trace of this in the half-century covered by the New Testament?)

The fact is that scripture contains neither a clear example of baptizing babies nor an exhortation to do it. The silence is deafening - and continues until the latter half of the second century. Even then, and for some time afterwards, it is clearly a matter of debate, even dispute. During the fourth and fifth centuries it became normal and remained so for the next thousand years, even when European "Christendom" split into the Orthodox east and the Catholic west. All through this period, however, there were some independent groups of Christians who kept to the original practice of believer's baptism; but they were small and persecuted.

Why was infant baptism (or, more accurately, baby baptism) introduced? Three reasons have been given and the answer may be a mixture of all three:

First, over the same period the church slipped back into some Old Testament ways. Priests, altars, vestments, incense and other "temple" features appeared almost as soon as Christians were allowed to erect their own buildings. It was perhaps inevitable that an equivalent of circumcision would follow.

Second, as the Roman Empire became generally and then officially "Christianized," ultimately giving way to "Christendom" (the kingdom of Christ), the distinction between church and state was increasingly blurred. Membership in the one and citizenship in the other became one and the same thing. A baby was considered born into both.

Third, and this was probably the main stimulus, it came to be believed and taught that baptism cleansed from "original" sin (inherited from Adam, along with his guilt), rather than washing away actual sins committed by the person themselves. Since babies are born with original sin, it followed that they would go to hell unless this was cleansed. In days when the infant mortality rate was exceptionally high by modern standards, it is understandable that parents wanted baptism for their babies as soon as possible. Indeed, in an emergency anyone could do it, provided they used some water and said the right words, namely the decreed Trinitarian formula. This harsh doctrine was later modified: unbaptized babies would only go to "limbus infantum" (limbo), but still could not be buried in "consecrated" ground. This has left a legacy of superstitious fear surrounding childbirth.

The "protesting" reformers of the sixteenth century switched from the (Catholic) church to the Bible as their authority in matters of belief and behaviour. They rejected many long-standing traditions which could not be supported from Scripture. The major reformers (Luther, Calvin and Zwingli) all soon realized that infant baptism was not biblical (Luther called it "unbeliever's baptism"!) – yet none of them abolished it. It was left to the more radical reformers (called "Anabaptists," which means "Twice-baptizers") to restore believer's baptism in practice. However, they were persecuted for it, even by Protestants, sometimes being drowned for it.

So what went wrong? Why did the Reformation get stuck at this point? The truth is that the reforms were carried through by legislation rather than evangelism. Whole cities and states were changed from Catholic to Protestant by order and example of the civic authorities. The medieval tie between church and State was too useful to be broken. The boundary between the two remained blurred; membership and citizenship were not clearly separated. Entry into both was by birth. So how was this justified from scripture by the "magisterial reformers" (i.e. those who used the power of the magistrate to bring about reform)?

Luther rather feebly argued that no one could tell if a baby is not a believer and babies may be presumed to have faith! Calvin (in Geneva) and Bullinger (in Zurich) found another way. Lumping together all the covenants in the Bible (including the "old" one of Moses and the "new" one of Christ) into one "covenant of grace," they then argued that just as Jews inherited the covenant of Abraham by being born of his flesh, Christian children did the same by being born of believing parents. Baptism and circumcision therefore have an identical purpose - a seal of recognition that the baby is already within "the covenant", by virtue of their parentage. Of course, circumcision leaves an indelible mark more appropriate to a "seal", whereas baptism does not and can be totally forgotten.

So the traditional practice was retained, but the rationale for it was changed. Theoretically, based on this new view, baptism should be strictly limited to babies whose parents have a saving knowledge of the Lord Jesus. It rarely is. Even "godparents" have been introduced to cover parental deficiencies.

More recently, yet another reason has been found for infant baptism. It is said that baptism expressed the "prevenient" (preceding) grace of God. To baptize babies expresses the fact that God loves them before they love him. He takes the initiative in saving them, even before they are aware of him. All this is true – but it has nothing to do with baptism!

Most churches "christening" babies have had to introduce a further rite called "confirmation", usually held at the onset of adulthood, when the now-grown child can "confirm" what was done for them by professing it for themselves. Such ceremonies are not needed when baptism is confined to penitent believers, as in the New Testament.

One thing is certain. Baptism cannot be applied to babies without radically changing its meaning. The three main reasons given to justify the practice (original sin, inherited covenant and prevenient grace) are not the New Testament grounds for a practice which combines a bath for the dirty and a burial for the dead.

This brief summary cannot possibly do justice to the various viewpoints and the reader may be referred to fuller treatments of the subject (among them, my study *The Normal Christian Birth*) and is encouraged to listen to others – but especially to the Holy Spirit through Scripture.

Two very practical questions remain:

First, what is to be done about those who come to repentance and faith, ask for baptism, but are refused because they were "christened" as a baby? This can cause tension and frustration on all sides.

Let it be said immediately that Christian baptism should not (indeed, cannot) be repeated. To be baptized a "second" time is therefore to deny the validity of the first. There can only be "one baptism" (Ephesians 4:5) in one life.

But that does not solve the problem. It changes the question to: What makes a baptism valid (in the sight of the Lord rather than the church)? Is it just what the baptizer does or is it dependent on the baptized as well? Are the water and the words enough or are repentance and faith vital ingredients?

While respecting the views of other Christians and churches, the answer must be sought from the Lord himself. This means searching the scriptures (all thirty passages about baptism in the New Testament), asking the Spirit of truth to say whether what is written about it has happened or not yet happened. He will not let you down, provided he is allowed to be the main influence on your thinking.

Second, what is to be done about children wanting to be baptized? Is there any age at which they can be considered to be ready?

The Jews set the age of twelve for assuming personal and spiritual responsibility. This can only be a guideline for Christian parents, but should make us cautious with any child below that age.

The real question is not age, but attitude and understanding. Surprisingly, this is easier to discern where the child receives opposition rather than encouragement in the home. A child with loving parents who love the Lord will naturally want to be like them.

Perhaps the key is to consider repentance, as well as faith. A child may be ready to say "Yes" to Jesus, but not yet ready to say "No" to the world, the flesh and the devil. Do they know, or even can they know, what they are turning down (for example, marriage to an unbeliever)? Many children brought up in a sheltered Christian environment and baptized very early break away when they reach their teens. After sampling the "far country", they realize their mistake and return to their childlike faith. Invariably, they want to be baptized again ("now I really know what I'm doing") and have to be refused. Baptism is not for those who are following their parents' faith, but for those who have found their own - for life.

Since it is a once-in-a-lifetime event, it would seem much better to be too slow rather than too quick. More harm is done by rushing than by waiting. The younger children are, the more careful we should be.

One final thought. Baptism should come before partaking in the Lord's Supper. If children are ready to take the bread and wine, they are ready to take to the water. Both sacraments are for penitent believers: the qualifications are the same.

For more of David Pawson's teaching,
including DVDs and CDs, go to
www.davidpawson.com

FOR FREE DOWNLOADS
www.davidpawson.org

www.ingramcontent.com/pod-product-compliance
Lightning Source LLC
Chambersburg PA
CBHW071029080526
44587CB00015B/2550